No Lex 1-13

"I would not exchange my color for all the wealth in the world, for had I been born white I might not have been able to do all that I have done or yet hope to do."

— MARY McLeod Bethune

MARY McLeod Bethune

By Amy Robin Jones

GRAPHIC DESIGN
Robert E. Bonaker / Graphic Design & Consulting Co.

PROJECT COORDINATOR
James R. Rothaus / James R. Rothaus & Associates

EDITORIAL DIRECTION
Elizabeth Sirimarco Budd

COVER PHOTO
Portrait of Mary McLeod Bethune
Schomburg Center for Research in Black Culture

Library of Congress Cataloging-in-Publication Data
Jones, Amy Robin, 1958-
Mary McLeod Bethune / Amy Robin Jones.
p. cm.
Includes bibliographical references and index.
Summary: A simple biography of the black educator who was
instrumental in creating opportunities for blacks in
education and government.
ISBN 1-56766-722-8 (library : reinforced : alk. paper)

1. Bethune, Mary McLeod, 1875-1955 — Juvenile literature.
2. Afro-American women — Biography — Juvenile literature.
3. Afro-Americans — Biography — Juvenile literature.
4. Teachers — United States — Juvenile literature. 5. Afro-
American women civil rights workers — Biography —
Juvenile literature. [1. Bethune, Mary McLeod, 1875-1955.
2. Teachers. 3. Afro-Americans — Biography. 4. Women —
Biography.] I. Title

E185.97.B34 J66 2000
370'.92 — dc21   99-045336
[B]

Contents

Seeking and Sharing Education

Mary McLeod Bethune stood and looked around her. A small shack stood in the middle of what was once a garbage dump. Bits of rubbish poked out of the ground. Pine trees and oaks baked in the hot sun. Mary saw all this, but she saw something more inside her own mind. She saw a large white building with windows. She saw young girls walking on sidewalks. She saw gardens. She saw students and teachers learning and sharing.

"It's $250," a man's voice broke into Mary's thoughts. She looked at the man standing beside her. Then she looked once more around the abandoned field. She smiled and said, "I'll bring you a **down payment.**"

What the man didn't know was that Mary had no down payment. She didn't have any money at all. But she did have a dream. She had started a small school for black girls in Daytona Beach, Florida. Now she wanted to expand that school. Mary had a long history of making dreams come true. She knew that dreams only came true through hard work and **perseverance.**

Bethune-Cookman College

BY 1907, MARY HAD RAISED ENOUGH MONEY TO BUILD A LARGE SCHOOLHOUSE. SHE CALLED THE BUILDING FAITH HALL, "PARTLY BECAUSE IT WAS AN EXAMPLE OF WHAT COULD BE BROUGHT ABOUT BY FAITH."

MARY MCLEOD BETHUNE HAD AN IMPORTANT GOAL:
SHE WANTED TO GIVE BLACK CHILDREN IN THE
UNITED STATES THE CHANCE TO GO TO SCHOOL.

Bethune-Cookman College

SUNDAY SCHOOL STUDENTS AT MARY'S SCHOOL POSE FOR A PHOTOGRAPH IN
1915. MARY (CIRCLED) STANDS AT THE LEFT WITH FOUR OTHER TEACHERS.

When Mary got home, she went straight to her kitchen. She baked all day and all night. She asked friends and students to help her. She sold ice cream and sweet-potato pies. Mary went to everyone she knew, and even some people she didn't know. She explained her dream of moving her small school from a four-room cottage to a large **campus.** By the end of the week, she had the down payment for the land — $5. She wrapped up the money in a handkerchief and brought it to the man.

The school continued to grow and grow. By 1915, the land was worth almost a million dollars. In 1923, the school merged with the Cookman Institute for Men in Jacksonville, Florida. It was renamed Bethune-Cookman College. Mary McLeod Bethune was the first black woman to start a college for black students. She was also the first black woman to be the president of a college.

MARY SERVED AS PRESIDENT OF BETHUNE-COOKMAN COLLEGE UNTIL 1942.

Bethune-Cookman College

Dreams and Determination

Education was always important to Mary. She was born on July 10, 1875, in Mayesville, South Carolina. At that time in the South, there were no schools for black children. Her mother, her father, and many of her brothers and sisters had been slaves. After the Civil War ended in 1865, the slaves were free. But life was still very difficult for the McLeod family and other **African Americans.**

The McLeods worked on their 35-acre farm. They grew cotton to earn money. They grew their own food to eat. They made almost everything else they needed. Even though she was young, Mary was a hard worker. She once boasted that at just nine years old, she could pick 250 pounds of cotton a day.

There was little time for play or to go to school. Even if there had been time, few black children had the chance to get an education. Black children in the South (and often in the North) were not allowed to go to classes with white children. Many people felt education was not necessary for the black community. Some even believed it was dangerous to educate blacks. Educated African Americans might begin to demand equal rights, and some people were afraid of that.

Even so, Sam and Patsy McLeod wanted one of their 17 children to get an education. In 1885, they picked Mary to go to Trinity Presbyterian Mission School. Mary woke early each morning, did her chores, and walked to school. She studied hard in her classes, walked home, and did more chores. Then each night, she taught her brothers and sisters all she had learned.

Bethune-Cookman College

MARY WAS BORN IN THIS SMALL CABIN IN 1875. SHE HAD
A LARGE FAMILY WITH MANY BROTHERS AND SISTERS.

CORBIS

FOR MANY YEARS AFTER THE CIVIL WAR, AFRICAN AMERICAN CHILDREN COULD NOT ATTEND SCHOOL. THEY WERE BUSY WORKING TO HELP THEIR PARENTS, LIKE THIS LITTLE BOY WHO WORKED ON A TOBACCO FARM. THERE ALSO WERE VERY FEW SCHOOLS AVAILABLE FOR BLACK CHILDREN.

Mary did so well in school that her teachers selected her to attend the Scotia **Seminary** in Concord, North Carolina. There she received religious training. She also received an industrial education. This meant she learned skills to help her find work, such as sewing, cooking, washing, and cleaning. But Mary also learned to speak and write with confidence and power. Finally she went to the Moody Bible Institute in Chicago.

The Moody Bible Institute sent **missionaries** to countries around the world. These people went to faraway places to teach religion and to help people. Sometimes the missionaries went to Africa. Mary dreamed of going there. Mary's mother was proud of being from Africa. She told her children everything she knew about the land of their **ancestors.** Mary wanted to help the African people. But she was to be terribly disappointed. The Moody Institute would not send black missionaries to Africa.

Mary had to find a new dream. She began teaching at the Haines Institute in Augusta, Georgia. Mary decided she would teach African Americans, just as she had taught her brothers and sisters. Her real mission would be to help American children receive an education.

Mary soon realized that the education most black students received was not very helpful. African American schools usually offered classes to help students be better servants or laborers. They did not teach African Americans to be leaders. Mary also realized that girls were rarely included in education plans. Mary intended to change that. She would teach black girls not only skills to find work, but also values to improve their lives.

Mary wanted to start her own school, but she was also busy with her family. She had earned enough money to pay the loan on her mother and father's farm. She had taught her sisters and brothers. She had cared for the many people around her. Now she wanted to start her own family.

Mary met Albertus Bethune and married him. Soon they had a little boy, named Albert. Mary loved her son very much. Still, she could not stay home full time to care for him. She knew she had other responsibilities.

Albertus found a job in Florida. The Bethune family moved, and Mary took her dream with her. In 1904, she started a small school in Daytona Beach, Florida. She called it the Daytona Normal and Industrial Institute.

Mary had only $1.50 to buy supplies for her classroom. For furniture, she used wooden crates. She used charred sticks for pencils and mashed berries for ink. Her class was made up of just five little girls. Their parents paid **tuition** of 50 cents each week. Soon four-year-old Albert was attending the school, too.

Mary was lucky to have such dreams and goals because her family life was not always easy. Her marriage was not happy. She and her husband spent more and more time apart. Finally, Mary and Albertus seperated. When Albert was older, he went away to school.

Mary continued to teach. She also worked hard to raise more money for her school. The people of Daytona Beach — both blacks and whites — offered to help. They gave her money, books, and furniture. Because of Mary's dedication, the school eventually grew to become a four-year college. Today the school she started is called Bethune-Cookman College.

MARY POSES FOR A PHOTOGRAPH WITH HER GROWN-UP SON, ALBERT. MARY ONCE SAID, "HAVING A CHILD MADE ME MORE THAN EVER DETERMINED TO BUILD BETTER LIVES FOR MY PEOPLE."

Bethune-Cookman College

Bethune-Cookman College

MARY'S DREAM WAS TO START A SCHOOL ESPECIALLY FOR AFRICAN AMERICAN GIRLS. WITH A LOT OF EFFORT, HER DREAM CAME TRUE. SHE CALLED HER SCHOOL THE DAYTONA NORMAL AND INDUSTRIAL INSTITUTE.

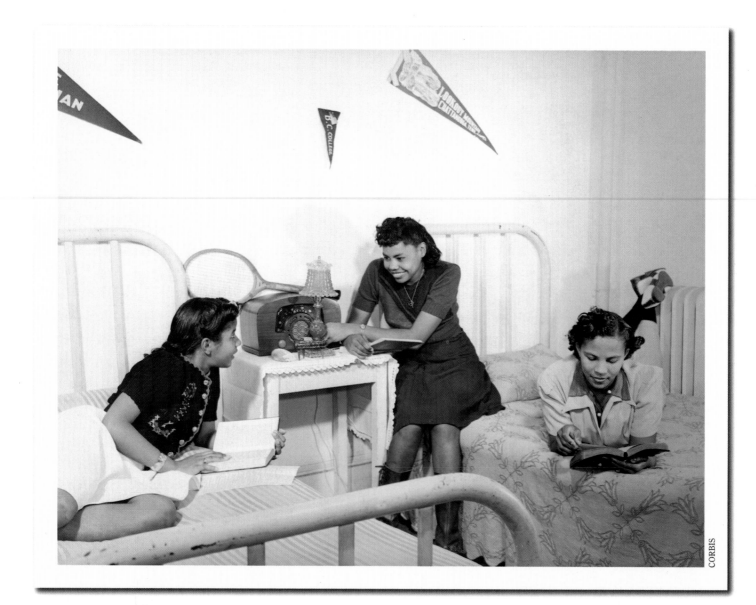

YOUNG WOMEN AT BETHUNE-COOKMAN COLLEGE SPEND TIME TOGETHER IN 1943.
MARY BELIEVED THAT AFRICAN AMERICAN WOMEN COULD DO ANYTHING IF THEY HAD
COURAGE, DETERMINATION, AND A GOOD EDUCATION.

The Woman's Era

Mary McLeod Bethune thought about the world's problems a lot. She believed one of the biggest problems was that women could not achieve their **potential.** "I am a believer in women and I believe in their possibilities," she said. Mary believed women could do more with their lives if they had the same opportunities men had.

Mary was always busy with the college. Still, she found time to work with other groups — especially those that helped women and African Americans. Mary strongly believed that black women could make a difference. They just had to cooperate and work together. She joined forces with other women who had the same ideas.

Mary and many women like her believed that African American women should care for their homes and families. But they should have other responsibilities, too. African American women could work to improve the lives of their people. From 1890 until 1940, black women all over the country joined groups that had been started to do just that. This period was known as the Woman's Era in African American history.

Mary joined a group called the National Association of Wage Earners (NAWE). The NAWE wanted to educate working black women. Black workers were usually paid less than white workers were. Sometimes employers fired African Americans without a good reason. Black workers were often given too much work to do in a single day. The NAWE believed black women deserved better wages and working conditions. They taught working women to fight for fair treatment.

Mary also joined the National Association of Colored Women (NACW). This group fought against **racism, sexism,** and **discrimination.** Its members worked to improve women's lives. The NACW was also one of the first groups to help support Mary's school.

By 1924, the NACW had more than 10,000 members. Mary had been a member for many years. Other members knew she was energetic, powerful, and intelligent. She worked hard, both to gain opportunities for women and to fight racism. She was also a gifted speaker and writer. When Mary spoke to people, she could move and inspire them. That year, Mary was voted president of the NACW.

At the time, the United States had many unfair laws that discriminated against African Americans. These **segregation** laws separated black and white people. Blacks could not use the same public facilities as whites. They could not attend the same churches, schools, or theaters. Blacks even had a difficult time voting in elections. Some white people threatened blacks who tried to vote.

Mary refused to accept this. She made people aware of these **policies.** She also worked hard to change them. She voted at every election she could. She even defied the threats of the **Ku Klux Klan.** This violent group often threatened to harm African Americans who tried to vote.

Mary had always fought discrimination. Many years before, a student at Bethune-Cookman College had become ill. Mary took her to a local hospital. The hospital staff segregated the girl from the white patients. What did Mary decide to do about it? She started her own hospital for African Americans in 1911. She named it after her father. Both black and white doctors worked at the McLeod Hospital, and all patients were treated equally.

CORBIS

MARY WAS A LEADER AMONG NATIONAL ORGANIZATIONS THAT HELPED WOMEN AND FOUGHT RACISM. MUCH OF HER TIME WAS SPENT ENCOURAGING OTHER WOMEN TO JOIN FORCES TO MAKE AMERICA A NATION OF EQUALITY AND JUSTICE.

CORBIS/Bettmann

MEMBERS OF THE NATIONAL ASSOCIATION OF COLORED WOMEN (NACW) PROTEST OUTSIDE THE WHITE HOUSE. THE NACW MOTTO WAS "LIFTING AS WE CLIMB." THIS MEANT THAT AS WOMEN "CLIMBED" TO IMPROVE THEIR OWN LIVES, THEY "LIFTED" OR HELPED OTHERS ALONG THE WAY.

Over the years, Mary continued to fight **injustice** every chance she got. Once she planned a dinner at the famous Waldorf-Astoria Hotel in New York City. The management would not serve her group. Mary refused to be treated that way. She would not move her party. Finally, the hotel manager agreed. Mary and all her guests enjoyed a wonderful dinner at the hotel.

In 1927, Mary went to a meeting of the National Council of Women (NCW). The NCW was a segregated organization. Mary went to represent the National Association of Colored Women. She walked into the home of Franklin Delano Roosevelt, who was the governor of New York at the time. His wife, Eleanor Roosevelt, was hosting the event.

There was a moment of silence as Mary entered. She was tall, confident, and intelligent. Still, many of the white women were **prejudiced** against African Americans. The Roosevelts were not. Sara Delano Roosevelt, Franklin's mother, took Mary by the arm. The two women sat next to each other. Like Mary, the Roosevelt family fought against racism in whatever way they could.

Mary soon became the friend and coworker of Eleanor Roosevelt. They were **allies** in the struggle for racial equality. Racism was still part of Mary's life, however. At a tea party, a white woman said, "Mrs. Bethune, it is wonderful of Mrs. Roosevelt to have you here." Mary replied, "It is great of her to have *all* of us here." Mary refused to be discriminated against, but she often handled such difficult situations with humor. She would need this quality, and all her strength, in the years to come.

A Time of Turmoil

Mary had been working with the NACW for some time. Unfortunately, she was not satisfied. The members in different states did not always communicate with each other. Mary decided to found a new organization, the National Council of Negro Women (the NCNW). This group would help organize and fund all black women's groups. Mary still had a vision of what African American women could accomplish if they worked together.

Mary's hard work was rewarded in 1935 when she received the Spingarn Medal. The National Association for the Advancement of Colored People (NAACP) awarded this honor for outstanding achievement by an African American. Mary was honored for her work as the founder and president of Bethune-Cookman College and her national leadership.

Franklin Roosevelt was elected U.S. president in 1932. He had met Mary through her work with Eleanor and Sara Roosevelt. In 1936, he asked Mary to work with him.

Mary worried about the United States. It had been gripped by the **Great Depression.** Many people had lost their jobs and could find no work. There were thousands of people without homes.

The Great Depression hit African Americans especially hard. Many government agencies that could help people had racist policies. Blacks were often discriminated against. Jobs were found for white workers first. Money was given to white people first, too. Only what was left over went to African Americans.

Mary McLeod Bethune Council House NHS/National Park Service

MARY MCLEOD BETHUNE RECEIVED MANY HONORS AND AWARDS DURING HER LIFETIME. PEOPLE RECOGNIZED HER DEDICATION AND COMPASSION.

MARY BETHUNE AND ELEANOR ROOSEVELT LED A NATIONAL YOUTH
ASSOCIATION (NYA) CONFERENCE. MARY'S FRIENDSHIP WITH THE
ROOSEVELT FAMILY CONTINUED TO STRENGTHEN OVER THE YEARS.
PRESIDENT ROOSEVELT NAMED MARY THE DIRECTOR OF THE
DIVISION OF NEGRO AFFAIRS FOR THE NYA.

Although Mary was an important American leader, she still faced racism. Some people called her names. They even tried to make her feel inferior. One evening, she was leaving an event at the White House. A southern politician asked her, "Auntie, what are you doing here?" (Some white southerners called older black servants "Auntie" or "Uncle.") She looked at him and replied, "Which one of my sister's children are you?" Even when she was angry, Mary used her sense of humor to make a point.

Mary knew the best way to fight racism was with intelligence. She could make a difference through her work with President Roosevelt. She helped create the president's policies on race and discrimination. She also organized a large meeting for the National Youth Administration (NYA). Many important people attended the meeting. They talked about the problems young black people faced.

Mary believed the most serious problems were unemployment, poverty, and homelessness. She thought young African Americans needed more places to go for recreation. Of course, she still believed that black Americans needed better schools. Mary worked closely with the NYA to achieve these goals.

President Roosevelt named Mary the director of the Division of Negro Affairs for the NYA. She started special programs for young African Americans. She also encouraged the government to help black students pay their tuition.

Because of Mary, black reporters were finally admitted to the White House for news briefings. She demanded that black doctors be allowed to work at Johns Hopkins Hospital in Maryland. Black nurses were finally allowed to work at Howard University's Freedmen's Hospital in Washington, D.C. Mary helped change all of these policies.

Mary also helped organize the Federal Council on Negro Affairs. This group worked to **recruit** black advisors into the government. The Council held two conferences (in 1937 and 1939), and Mary was in charge of them. When arguments or difficulties arose, Mary's strength helped. She would say, "Let's now have prayer." The room would grow quiet as her voice rose in a hymn. Her religious **convictions** gave her confidence and power to lead others.

As Mary worked to solve problems in her own country, problems outside the United States were growing. The whole world was in **turmoil.** Europe was at war. It looked as if the United States would soon follow.

In 1941, the United States entered the war when Japan bombed Pearl Harbor in Hawaii. During World War II, the NYA organized a program to train pilots. Mary made sure that six black colleges offered this program to students. After this training, black **aviators** were able to fly military airplanes.

Thousands of African Americans fought to protect their country, but they were treated unfairly. The U.S. **armed forces** were segregated. Black soldiers could not fight in the same units as white soldiers. They seldom attained important jobs in the armed forces. This upset many people. There were even city **riots** because African Americans were so angry at this injustice. During the war, Mary constantly protested against segregation and other racist practices in the armed forces.

During World War II, women were not allowed to join the armed forces. Instead, they could join other military organizations such as the Women's Army Corps (WAC) or the Army Nurse Corps. These groups did not allow African Americans to join. Mary fought against these policies, too.

CORBIS

WORLD WAR II CREATED MANY JOBS IN THE UNITED STATES. THE GOVERNMENT NEEDED WORKERS TO BUILD MANY THINGS, SUCH AS WEAPONS, TOOLS, BOATS, AIRPLANES, AND TANKS. STUDENTS AT BETHUNE-COOKMAN COLLEGE TRAINED FOR SUCH JOBS. MARY MADE SURE THAT THE COLLEGE TAUGHT IMPORTANT SKILLS TO HELP THE STUDENTS FIND WORK.

Mary wrote an important essay called *Certain Unalienable Rights*. In this essay, she explained what African Americans wanted:

"What does the Negro want? The answer is very simple. He wants only what all other Americans want. He wants opportunity to make real what the Declaration of Independence and the Constitution and the Bill of Rights say, what the four freedoms establish. While he knows these ideals are open to no man completely, he wants only his equal chance to obtain them."

Thanks to Mary's effort, black women were finally allowed to serve in the WAC. Mary was named the special assistant to the Secretary of War. She was responsible for choosing black WAC **officer** candidates. These women would be leaders who helped make important decisions for the corps. Mary's hard work had paid off.

MARY IN HER WOMEN'S ARMY CORPS (WAC) UNIFORM DURING WORLD WAR II. AT FIRST, AFRICAN AMERICAN WOMEN COULD NOT JOIN THE WAC. MARY FOUGHT AGAINST THIS POLICY UNTIL ALL RACES COULD CONTRIBUTE THEIR SKILLS TO THE CORPS.

Bethune-Cookman College

CORBIS/Bettmann

MARY GREETS TWO YOUNG RECRUITS AT A WOMEN'S ARMY CORPS TRAINING CAMP. IN 1942, THE U.S. GOVERNMENT PERMITTED AFRICAN AMERICAN WOMEN TO JOIN THE WAC.

A Legacy of Civil Rights

Mary was an important force in the world of politics. She was a respected leader. She was the first black woman appointed to the **cabinet** of a U.S. president. She had power. She was well known. But she never let go of her first dream. She always reminded African Americans that education was the best way to fight poverty and hardship. She served as a role model for women. She was not only a loving mother, she also had a busy and successful career.

When the war was over, Mary was tired. She had health problems, and her doctor warned her to rest. She tried to slow down, but it was impossible. She was needed. In 1945, she served as **consultant** at a conference to draft a United Nations Charter. President Truman appointed her to a defense committee. She still worked to make Bethune-Cookman College the best it could be.

Mary lived in a house on the college campus. She kept a collection of elephants made from wood, clay, and other materials. She also kept a walking stick that once belonged to Franklin D. Roosevelt and the crystal given to her by the millionaire John D. Rockefeller.

Mary was still active. She had a special dress made of black velvet with the necklace and bracelets sewn on to it. She said this saved her time when she dressed because she didn't have to worry about jewelry. But she knew she did not have much time left.

IN 1948, PRESIDENT TRUMAN SIGNED A BILL TO CREATE "NATIONAL FREEDOM DAY" IN HONOR OF THE 13TH AMENDMENT TO THE CONSTITUTION. THIS IMPORTANT AMENDMENT OUTLAWED SLAVERY IN THE UNITED STATES FOREVER. MARY (THIRD FROM LEFT) AND OTHER AFRICAN AMERICAN LEADERS WERE THERE TO TAKE PART IN THE OCCASION.

Bethune-Cookman College

AFTER WORLD WAR II, MARY TRIED TO LIVE A QUIETER LIFE. BUT SHE STILL DEDICATED HER TIME TO THE THINGS THAT WERE IMPORTANT TO HER — ESPECIALLY BETHUNE-COOKMAN COLLEGE.

Mary knew she had accomplished a great deal. She also knew there was much more left to do. She had already written important articles and letters. Now she wanted to remind people that "equality for the Negro" had not yet been reached. She wrote a final document when she was 78 years old. In "My Last Will and Testament," Mary wrote:

I leave you the challenge of developing confidence in one another.

I leave you a thirst for education.

I leave you a respect for the uses of power.

I leave you faith.

I leave you dignity.

I leave you a desire to live harmoniously with your fellow men.

I leave you. . . a responsibility to our young people.

Mary died at age 79, soon after writing "My Last Will and Testament." She had a heart attack on May 18, 1955. It was an important year in African American history. That December, a woman named Rosa Parks was arrested after she refused to give up her bus seat to a white man in Alabama. People all over the country began to fight against injustice. They began to protest against discrimination and racism. The battle for **civil rights** was growing stronger than ever as Mary McLeod Bethune left the life, country, and people she loved.

Mary McLeod Bethune was one of the most powerful African American women of the 20th century. She had strong religious convictions. Mary was a role model for other women. She was committed to uplifting African Americans through education, civil rights, and political power. She encouraged black women to reach their full potential.

She is also one of the people remembered during **Kwanzaa** and Black History Month. Schools are named after her. Her home on the Bethune-Cookman campus is a National Historic Landmark. A bronze statue was erected in 1974 to honor her. It shows Mary, leaning on her walking cane, passing on her will to two children. The statue is on Capitol Hill in Washington, D.C.

But most important are her legacy of love, her focus on education and opportunity, and her determination to make her own dreams come true. "Most people think I am a dreamer," she once said. "Through dreams many things have come true."

Mary McLeod Bethune Council House NHS/National Park Service

IN 1943, MARY MCLEOD BETHUNE AND THE NATIONAL COUNCIL OF NEGRO WOMEN BOUGHT A HOUSE IN WASHINGTON, D.C., TO BE THE ORGANIZATION'S HEADQUARTERS. TODAY THE HOUSE IS A MUSEUM HONORING THE HISTORY OF AFRICAN AMERICAN WOMEN.

Mary McLeod Bethune Council House NHS/National Park Service

Timeline

1875	Mary McLeod is born in Mayesville, South Carolina, on July 10.
1885	Mary starts school at the Trinity Presbyterian Mission School. Of the McLeod family's 17 children, only Mary is able to attend school. In the evenings, she teaches her brothers and sisters what she has learned in class.
1890	The "Women's Era" begins, and African American women around the country join clubs and groups to improve the lives of their people. The Women's Era in African American history is said to be the period between 1890 and 1940.
1893	Mary graduates from Scotia Seminary.
1895	Mary graduates from the Moody Bible Institute in Chicago.
1904	Mary founds Daytona Normal and Industrial Institute for Girls in Daytona Beach, Florida.
1923	The Daytona Institute merges with Cookman Institute of Jacksonville. It is now called Bethune-Cookman College. Mary serves as the college president until 1942.
1935	The National Association for the Advancement of Colored People awards Mary the Spingarn Medal. Mary founds the National Council of Negro Women and begins working with the National Youth Association.
1939	Mary becomes the director of the Division of Negro Affairs of the National Youth Administration.
1941	The United States enters World War II. Thousands of African American soldiers fight to protect their country throughout the war.
1942	The Women's Army Corps (WAC) begins enlisting women for duties outside combat. Mary fights the WAC's policy of not accepting African American women. She is later responsible for choosing black WAC officer candidates.
1945	Mary is a consultant at the Conference to Draft a United Nations Charter.
1948	President Truman establishes "National Freedom Day" to honor the 13th Amendment. Mary and other African American leaders are present to witness the occasion.
1954	Mary writes "My Last Will and Testament."
1955	Mary dies at age 79 in her home on the Bethune-Cookman College campus.
1974	Mary's house on the Bethune-Cookman College campus is named a National Historic Landmark.

Glossary

African Americans (AF-rih-kun uh-MAYR-ih-kunz)
African Americans are black Americans whose ancestors came from Africa. Mary McLeod Bethune was an African American.

allies (AL-eyz)
Allies are people, groups, or nations that work together toward a common goal. Mary Bethune and Eleanor Roosevelt were allies in the fight against racism and discrimination.

ancestors (AN-ses-terz)
Ancestors are someone's family members who were born long before, such as a grandparents or great grandparents. Mary's ancestors were from Africa.

armed forces (ARMD FOR-sez)
The armed forces are groups of soldiers that protect a nation. In the United States, the armed forces are the Army, the Navy, the Air Force, and the Marine Corps.

aviators (AY-vee-ay-terz)
Aviators are airplane pilots. Some African American soldiers were aviators in World War II.

cabinet (KA-bih-net)
A cabinet is a group of people that offers advice to a president or ruler. Mary McLeod Bethune was the first African American woman to be appointed to a U.S. president's cabinet.

campus (KAM-pes)
A campus includes the buildings and grounds of a school, college, or university. The Bethune-Cookman College campus is in Daytona, Florida.

civil rights (SIV-el RYTZ)
Civil rights are the personal freedoms that belong to all citizens of the United States. The Constitution guarantees civil rights.

consultant (kun-SULL-tent)
A consultant is a person, usually an expert at something, who is hired to give advice to an organization. The United Nations asked Mary Bethune to be a consultant.

convictions (KUN-VIK-shunz)
Convictions are strong opinions or beliefs about something. Mary Bethune had strong convictions about religion, education, and equality.

discrimination (dis-krim-ih-NAY-shun)
Discrimination is the unfair treatment of people (such as preventing them from getting jobs, or going to school) simply because they are different. African Americans have suffered discrimination by whites.

down payment (DOWN PAY-ment)
A down payment is the first payment made when buying something. Mary McLeod Bethune made a $5 down payment for the land where she built her school.

Great Depression (GRATE dee-PREH-shun)
The Great Depression was a period beginning in 1929 during which most Americans had very little money. Many people lost their jobs and could not support themselves or their families.

injustice (in-JUSS-tis)
An injustice is something that is unfair or takes away a person's rights. It was an injustice to treat black soldiers differently than white soldiers.

Ku Klux Klan (KOO KLUX KLAN)
The Ku Klux Klan is a group that discriminates against people who are not white and Christian. They are known to threaten people or commit acts of violence.

Glossary

Kwanzaa (KWAHN-zah)
Kwanzaa is a special winter holiday celebrated by African Americans. During Kwanzaa, African Americans remember their history and the traditions of their ancestors.

missionaries (MISH-uhn-ayr-eez)
Missionaries are people who teach their religion to others, often in another country. Mary wanted to go to Africa as a missionary.

officer (OFF–ih–ser)
An officer is a person in the military who leads others. Mary McLeod Bethune helped select officers for the Women's Army Corps.

perseverance (purr-se-VEER-entz)
Perseverance is the act of trying very hard to accomplish something. Mary McLeod Bethune knew that perseverance could make her dreams come true.

policies (PAWL-ih-seez)
Policies are rules and regulations about ways to do something. Mary McLeod Bethune helped President Roosevelt set his policies about race.

potential (poh-TEN-shel)
Potential is what a person is capable of achieving with his or her talent and intellect. Mary McLeod Bethune believed that society did not allow women to reach their full potential.

prejudiced (PREH-juh-dist)
People who are prejudiced have negative feelings or opinions about other people without good reason. Some white people are prejudiced against blacks.

racism (RAY-sih-zim)
Racism is a negative feeling or opinion about people because of their race. Racism can be committed by individuals, large groups, or even governments.

recruit (ree-KREWT)
If someone recruits other people, he or she encourages them join a group. Mary helped recruit black advisors into government jobs.

riots (RY-etz)
Riots are large, disorganized protests by many people in a public place. A riot usually starts because people are angry about something.

segregation (seg-rih-GAY-shun)
Segregation is actions and laws that separate people from one another. Segregation laws separated blacks and whites in the South for many years.

seminary (SEM-ih-nayr-ee)
A seminary is a type of school. Mary McLeod Bethune attended the Scotia Seminary as a young girl.

sexism (SEX-izm)
Sexism is a negative feeling or opinion about someone of the opposite sex. Sexism can mean that men think they are better than women or that women think they are better than men.

tuition (too-IH-shen)
Tuition is a fee for attending a school. Tuition to Mary Bethune's first school was 50 cents per week.

turmoil (TER-moyl)
Turmoil is a state of great difficulty or confusion. The world was in turmoil during World War II.

$\mathcal{I}ndex$

Further Information

Books

Flake, Sharon. *The Skin I'm In.* New York: Hyperion Press, 1998.

Greene, Carol. *Mary McLeod Bethune: Champion for Education.* Danbury, CT: Children's Press, 1993.

Haskins, James. *Separate but Not Equal: The Dream and the Struggle.* New York: Scholastic Trade, 1998.

Kelso, Richard. *Building a Dream: Mary Bethune's School (Stories of America).* Austin, TX: Raintree/Steck Vaughn, 1992.

McLoone, Margo. *Mary McLeod Bethune.* Mankato, MN: Capstone Press, 1997.

Web Sites

Hear Mary McLeod Bethune speak:
http://web.nypl.org/research/sc/scl/bethune.html

Visit Bethune-Cookman College:
http://www.bethune.cookman.edu/

Visit the Mary McLeod Bethune Council House:
http://www.nps.gov/mamc/

Tour National Historic sites that celebrate African American history:
http://www.cr.nps.gov/aahistory/